Becca Goes Batty

written and illustrated by
Larissa Ann Symbouras

Acknowledgments

To Eric, who always tells me I can do anything (except sing or whistle, and let's face it, you're not wrong) and pushes me to do it, do it right, and be my best, thank you. You're an amazing teammate. I also need to thank Cara, Dan, Avery, and Griffin, for your time, effort, expertise, editing help, critiques, and suggestions. Your perspective was absolutely invaluable, and you're all terrific! Thank you also to Joeleen, James, Nate, Luke, Christina, and Mitch and his kids, who took the time to read my story and give awesome insight. I so appreciate all of you. Thanks to Shannon for teaching me some wonderful new things about giraffes. Last, but definitely not least, thank you to Paige and Erika, who gave me the push to try this, and without whom this book wouldn't even exist.

Becca loved animals. All animals. Well, okay, almost all animals.

Becca loved her various pets, and almost all other animals, but was embarrassed to admit that there was one animal she didn't love. She was scared of bats! Her parents told her it was silly, and she knew that was true, but she just couldn't help it. When bats appeared in the dusk sky, all she wanted to do was duck and run into the house!

And then ...

... early one spring Saturday morning, Becca's mom came into her room with a letter.

"What's that?" asked Becca?

"It's addressed to you!" replied her mom.

To Becca

Dear Becca,

We've never had a visit with you,
and we're feeling a bit lonely here at the zoo.

We're inviting you to come and play
at the flying fox display!

You'll see how lovable we are,
and how great - the coolest by far!

Your friends,
The Flying Foxes

Sure enough, the envelope had

    To Becca

written on it. Curious, Becca opened it. Inside was a single sheet of paper.

    Dear Becca,

    We've never had a visit with you,
    and we're feeling a bit lonely here at the zoo.

    We're inviting you to come and play
    at the flying fox display!

    You'll see how lovable we are,
    and how great – the coolest by far!

    Your friends,
    The Flying Foxes

"Well," said Becca's mom. "I don't suppose we can refuse an invitation like that. Sounds like we're going to the zoo this afternoon!"

When she heard the word "zoo," Becca got excited. Flying foxes? Real foxes that could fly? Becca was skeptical, but definitely excited at the prospect of meeting them, and seeing for herself.

"Hey, mom? Can Griffin come with us too?" Griffin was Becca's best friend, who lived across the street, and who also loved animals. She just knew he'd want to meet these amazing foxes too.

"Let me call Griffin's mom and see," said mom.

Becca could hardly wait, rushed through her morning chores, and scarfed down her lunch so they could leave faster. Since Griffin's mom had said yes, they picked him up on their way out. While traveling to the zoo, Becca told him all about the letter she'd received that morning.

When they finally got there, Becca was jumping up and down against the seat belt, until her dad parked the car and mom opened the back door to let her and Griffin out. They got their tickets, passed through the big gate, and started at the first enclosure, a sensible place to start, where they found some American black bears playing.

"Look at the bears!" exclaimed Becca. "They look like they're having such fun, but I bet they're ferocious in the wild."

The bears stopped playing for a minute, and one said,

"Don't be silly!
We're not Grizzlies!
Our Alaskan cousins are the ones who hunt,
while most people we won't confront.
Black bears come out when you're not around.
Near lakes and rivers we'll be found.
We eat insects, nuts, and berries ...
also grubs, fish, and cherries!
If you leave it out, we'll get your trash,
grab it like take-out, and be off in a flash!"

"Well!" said Becca. "I don't know about eating bugs and trash, but the rest actually sounds pretty good!"

They all walked on, arriving at the bobcat habitat.

"They're so pretty!" exclaimed Becca. "I love those ears and spots! They're not that big; I wonder if they'd make good pets."

"I bet they would!" agreed Griffin.

One of the bobcats padded over to be closer to the children.

"We live in swamps, deserts, and woods,
And even pretty close to human neighborhoods.
But we need to be free to hunt for our meals.
It's animals, insects, and fish that appeal.
We're stealthy hunters who leap up to ten feet,
to get our paws onto what we will eat.
House cats we're not, it would be a bad plan
so as for being a pet, I don't think we can."

"That's fair," answered Becca.

"We'll just have to come visit you here instead!" added Griffin.

The bobcat nodded graciously, and with that, the children and Becca's parents walked on, enjoying the sun. Becca climbed a big rock near the path, hoping to get a view of the flying foxes, but with all the trees and buildings, she couldn't see very far into the zoo yet, so they all kept going.

Soon, they came upon skunks!

"I know everyone gets nervous around them because they spray that awful smell, but I think they're adorable, and would love to hug one," said Becca. The fluffiest skunk approached the family, and squeaked,

"Well, thanks! You're cute too!
Glad you're here at the zoo!

We also don't like the musk that we spray;
it's only to keep any danger away.
We won't spray the musk in a small space,
but if we're out in the open, we've got an eighteen foot range.
It's really just a last resort,
if our growling and hissing will not thwart
an enemy who's hanging around.
It's our best defense after those sounds.

If you see us about, standing tall with tail in the air,
don't be afraid, you don't need to be scared.
That's just a warning, but move on soon,
because after that, if we curl into a U,
you could be in for some smelly spray
so you should just try to back away."

"Wow, I had no idea even you didn't like the smell!" said Becca. She and Griffin agreed they'd be careful to watch the body language of any skunks they came across after this.

Continuing down the zoo's path, Griffin, Becca, and her parents came to the pond, inhabited by a whole flamboyance of flamingos, and a visiting duck or two.

"Look at how pink they are!" exclaimed Becca. "So pretty! And this one I know – they're pink because of the salmon they eat!" The nearest flamingo turned to her and studied her haughtily for a minute before saying,

"As it happens, that's a myth.
We don't eat salmon when we eat fish.
Our food is small and found in the mud.
We eat shrimp and algae, shellfish and bugs.
We use our bills upside-down, to scoop it up,
filter it on our tongues, which are covered in fluff.
Well, not really fluff, but it's definitely hairy.
So we don't get muddy food, at least not very.
It's something in the plankton that makes us pink.
It's called beta carotene, and keeps us healthy, I think."

"Wow! I had no idea! Can I ask one more question?" asked Becca, and the flamingo looked at her again, impatient. "Why do you stand on one leg so often, like when you eat?"

"That's our secret, and I'm not telling,
although the reason's quite compelling."

And with that, standing on one leg indeed, the flamingo dipped her head upside-down into the pond to continue eating. Becca's eyebrows raised at the flamingo's rudeness, but she decided to let it go, and continue enjoying her day with her friend and parents.

"Flamingos are definitely pretty," Becca's mom commented, "but a little too impressed with themselves, I think."

Farther down the path, the group happened upon a cluster of absolutely delightful – and huge – furry animals. Becca's eyes grew large. "Mom, dad, what are those?! It's like we fed the guinea pigs too much and they exploded!"

"We are capybaras," said the youngest one,
"Compared to guinea pigs, we nearly weigh a ton!

It makes sense we look like them to your widened eyes,
since, like them, we're cavies, though of extreme size.
We're obviously much bigger, over four feet long,
and love the water, we can stay all the way under for the length of a song!
Our feet are webbed, and we can swim,
to escape our predators, or just on a whim."

Becca was impressed. "My guinea pigs definitely aren't swimmers," she said, "and they're not even one foot long! It's so cool that you're their relatives!"

They moved on to the next habitat, where they found some tall, graceful giraffes! "How come they never make any sounds?" asked Becca, tilting her head waaaaay back to look up at a really tall one eating leaves from the top of a tree.

"I don't think giraffes talk," replied Griffin.

"That's ridiculous! Of course we talk!
We can talk as well as we walk!
What we do
may seem strange to you,
because you can't hear what we discuss,
but it's all perfectly natural to us.

We chat using something called 'infrasound,'
with which we have conversations that are profound.
Sounds too low for you to hear
with your unsophisticated ear."

"Oh, cool!" Becca called back to the giraffe, really glad she'd come to the zoo today and learned so many new things. But still, she couldn't wait to meet the foxes that flew, which were somewhere ahead.

"Dad, where are the flying foxes? I haven't seen a sign for them anywhere."

"I'm not sure, honey. We'll find them, I promise. How about we get some ice cream on the way?"

But Becca wasn't able to forget the flying foxes, even while she and Griffin enjoyed their chocolate-vanilla swirl cones with rainbow sprinkles.

She wanted to hurry along, but couldn't resist stopping at the next habitat, where she, Griffin, and her parents saw some absolutely captivating hippopotamuses with their babies, heading for the water.

"That water looks deep!" commented Becca. "Mom, do you think the little ones will be okay in there?"

The youngest of the hippos turned to Becca, and called,

> "We're built for water, don't worry 'bout us!
> My nose is on top, so there's no need to fuss.
>
> Back in Africa, the river's our home.
> With our eyes, nose, and ears on top of our dome,
> we can stand on the bottom and not miss any fun!
> It protects us from heat, and even the sun.
>
> We can breathe, hear, and see no matter what,
> while all down the river we prance and we strut."

"Oh, good," Becca called back. "Have fun!"

The group kept going, enjoying the warm, sunny afternoon, Becca thinking about the interesting animals she'd met so far, and still looking forward to these crazy foxes she hadn't yet seen. She was so lost in thought that she almost ran right into a fence, beyond which were a whole bunch of the most engaging animals she'd ever seen, each with big black patches around their eyes and exactly thirteen black and white rings on their long tails. The critters were all over, walking and sitting on the ground, on rocks, on logs, and high above, hanging from tree branches too, by their tails!

"Monkeys?" wondered Becca.

"Monkeys?! No, lemurs! We're rarer, by far.
Though they are our cousins, we're found only in Madagascar.
We're primates, so we're related, to be sure,
but we're also like humans, though the link's more obscure!"

"Wow!" replied Becca, excited at the prospect of being related to such amazing creatures.

Griffin added, "But ... um ... well ... not to be insulting ... but have you noticed kind of a strong smell around here?"

The biggest lemur replied, "We won't take offense,
They're the sign of a leader, and we're proud of our scents!
We mark every corner to claim this as home,
we scent for defense, and let it be known."

"Oh, good," said Griffin. "I'm glad you don't mind, and even more glad I didn't offend you."

Becca skipped down the cobblestone path ahead of her parents and Griffin, curly pigtails bouncing, past blooming dandelions buzzing with happy bees.

"Not so far ahead," called mom, "wait for us!"

Becca slowed down to let Griffin and her parents catch up, and together, they reached her dad's favorite animal, a herd of zebras. "I love their black stripes!," commented Becca, racing her dad to the fence for a closer look.

There was apparently one zebra a bit out of sorts,
because when he heard that, he was quick to retort,

"Actually, young lady, our stripes are not black.
What you see adorning all of my back
are stripes that are white, it's the black that's the base
I've worn them since birth, so I know that's the case.
No two are the same, there are no others like mine
That's how my friends know me, by my stripey design.
When lions come hunting, stripes also protect us.
When we stand close together, they cannot detect us."

"Well, that's handy!" Becca and her dad said at the same time, and then laughed. Dad beat Becca to the "jinx!"

The next area was huge! It had to be, considering the size of the animals it housed. These were the African elephants!

"I love elephants," said Becca, who we know loved almost all animals. "They seem like they know how to do so many things with their trunks!"

At that, the biggest baby elephant replied,

"They're even more useful than you think.
The trunk is our nose, plus we use it to drink.
Our trunks have 100,000 muscles too,
which means there are loads of things we can do.
We can grab things with the two fingers at the end,
like the leaves and grass we eat, my new friend.

Like dolphins and chimps, we're smart, it is true,
And we feel emotions, just like you do.
We're happy and sad, and we can be funny.
We have compassion for others and help them feel sunny.
Our parents raise us and teach us what they know.
Just like you kids, we learn what they show."

Becca and Griffin were surprised that elephants were so much like people. They hadn't known that. "Wow, you're just like us," said Becca, "We'll be back to visit you again soon!"

Looking ahead, Becca saw a sign that pointed to the right, and said, "Flying Foxes." "Look!" she exclaimed. "They're coming up soon!"

First, though, she stopped at a nearby enclosure. Becca commented, "Huge birds! They don't look like they could fly like that."

"I'm an emu, one of the largest birds on Earth.
I'm over six feet and have a wide girth.
As an emu, I cannot fly through the air
but I run really quickly, not many compare.
I can run up to thirty miles per hour.
Big though I am, my legs have that power.
If I ran as fast as I could near a school,
I'd get a ticket for speeding, for breaking the rules."

"Wow," said Griffin, "you'd do great in my gym class! I'm a pretty fast runner myself, but not like that!"

Across from the emus, since this was the Australian area of the zoo, was another enclosure, with a sign that read "Red Kangaroos."

"Hi, Kangaroos," called Becca! "Are you fast, like the emus too?" The nearest responded,

"Well hello, little girl, and welcome to the zoo,
I am even faster than the emu!
Thirty-five miles an hour, though I don't really run.
I jump high and far, I'm second to none,
twenty-five feet forward in one single leap,
and up six feet high when I'm at the peak."

"Wow!" exlaimed Becca, amazed at the abilities of the kangaroos.

As it happened, the animals right next to the kangaroos were also Australian marsupials, and Griffin's favorite. "Koalas!" he exclaimed, happily. "They're soooooooooooo cuuuuuuuuuuuuuuuuuuuuuute,"

"They are!" agreed Becca, "but not very playful, are they? Do they sleep during the day, and wake up at night?" She thought about the difference between these and the lemurs they'd seen earlier, and then couldn't help from wondering which the flying foxes would be like.

"You mean are they nocturnal?" asked mom. "No, I don't think so."

A baby koala, comfy in it's mommy marsupial's pouch, answered her,

> "It's not a matter of sleeping by day.
> We're pretty lazy in general, you could say.
> This is caused by our diet.
> It keeps our lives pretty quiet.
> We eat eucalyptus, it's our primary food;
> And honestly, we're pretty shrewd.
> Other species don't want any part of the stuff,
> so we don't have to compete to have enough.
> Of course that's because it's low in protein and hard to digest,
> or maybe 'cause it's poisonous for other species to ingest.
> Our slow metabolism means it's fine for us,
> but also that we're as slow-moving as a tortoise!"

From the enclosure across the way, Griffin, Becca, and her parents heard an insulted, "Hey!" and turned around, coming face to face with an actual tortoise, who had taken offense to the koala's comment. She carried her baby on her back.

"I'll have you know between the tortoise and hare,
the tortoise won the race, fair and square.
But that tortoise was steady and slow,
and you've no idea how fast I can go.
It just so happens you can't lump us all together.
It's true most are slow, but I, however,
am a pancake tortoise; I'm quick and I'm spry,
I'm agile and and lightweight, so don't even try
to say I'm the same as all of the others.
I'm really different; I'm one whiz of a runner.

Their shells are bulbous, solid, and allow them to hide,
so when faced with danger, they retreat inside.
Mine's flat and flexible, and full of holes.
It enables me to flee in the face of my foes,
into a desert rock crevice of my dry habitat.
So what do you all think about that?"

The koalas seemed a little embarrassed about having insulted their neighbor, the pancake tortoise. It wasn't really their fault, as pancake tortoises are from Africa, not Australia, and the koalas didn't know any better. The children and Becca's parents offered a quick goodbye, turned a corner, and ...

... had finally reached the building with the plaque saying "Flying Fox" on the outside! Excited to see these foxes that fly, Becca gave a shout and raced in ahead of Griffin and her parents, but stopped short, cringing, when what she saw in the dim light were ...

BATS!

"Bats?!" exclaimed Becca. "Flying foxes are bats?!"

"They are," responded her dad, catching up to her. "They're a type of bat that looks like a fox with wings."

"But they were so nice in their letter," said Becca. "I didn't think bats could be so nice. I don't know about this," she mumbled nervously.

Her mom volunteered, "It's OK. See how precious they are? They won't hurt you. Talk to them and see!"

Griffin nodded encouragement, so Becca turned to the bats warily and said, "You really are pretty cute up close. I hope you're not upset that I'm so surprised. My parents told me that bats eat mosquitoes, so I should like you. Is that true? Do you eat bugs?"

"Oh, those are our cousins, the insectivore bats.
They're the ones who eat meals like that.
It's true they live here, all over the States
and they help to control your insect pest rates.
Next time you see them, be sure to wave and say, 'Hey!'
Pass along our greeting at the dusk of the day.

We, on the other hand, are known as fruit bats.
In Europe, Africa, Asia, and Australia we hang our hats.
We're megabats, being bigger than most,
and we have important jobs from coast to coast.
When we eat our fruit meals, you see,
we naturally pollinate each fruit tree,
ensuring that flowers continue to bloom
so the land is filled with their sweet perfume.

While we're at it, when we drop bits while we feed,
we fly all over and spread lots of seeds.
When you visit a forest that knocks off your socks,
give credit to us, your friendly flying fox!

Bug eater or fruit bat, there's no need to fear ..."
(and here he broke off, and let out a cheer -)
"Oh, look! Feeding time! The keepers are here!"